T0130407

YOU ARE MAGNIFICENT JUST BE YOU

INSPIRATION TO MY YOUNG KINGZ & QUEENZ

Written and Illustrated By Terrica Booker

Copyright © 2020 Terrica Booker.

All rights reserved. No part of this book may be used or reproduced by any means,
graphic, electronic, or mechanical, including photocopying, recording, taping or by
any information storage retrieval system without the written permission of the author
except in the case of brief quotations embodied in critical articles and reviews.

Balboa Press books may be ordered through booksellers or by contacting:

Balboa Press
A Division of Hay House
1663 Liberty Drive
Bloomington, IN 47403
www.balboapress.com
844-682-1282

Because of the dynamic nature of the Internet, any web addresses or links contained
in this book may have changed since publication and may no longer be valid. The views
expressed in this work are solely those of the author and do not necessarily reflect the views
of the publisher, and the publisher hereby disclaims any responsibility for them.

Any people depicted in stock imagery provided by Getty Images are models,
and such images are being used for illustrative purposes only.
Certain stock imagery © Getty Images.

ISBN: 978-1-9822-5193-2 (sc)
ISBN: 978-1-9822-5192-5 (e)

Library of Congress Control Number: 2020913832

Print information available on the last page.

Balboa Press rev. date: 08/18/2020

BALBOA.PRESS

KINGZ & QUEENZ

This book was written to show our African American youth appreciation. In today's society and generation many young African Americans think they have no voice. This book is for them to understand that life may be different for them but to never give up. They are strong and to believe in themselves.

This book is meant to uplift their spirts and visions of changing the world. This book is to visualize how they are the future. This book is demonstrating how they shouldn't be ashamed of themselves. They are beautiful. This book is for them to love themselves for who they are. This book is to deliver them the message "THEY DO MATTER." You Are Magnificent. Just Be You.

Terrica Booker

HAIR

Your hair is as wavy as the waves of the roaring ocean. Your hair flows to the rhythm of the beat. Never let your hair define who you are. Wear those natural styles loud and proud. Show off those beautiful curls, twists, dread locks, braids, and Afro puffs.

EYES

Your eyes are as bright as the sunny sunset. Create a vision of empowerment, investment, and manifestation. Have focus, leadership mentality, and visualization of changing the world.

TEETH

Your teeth are as white as the pearls in the sea. Always smile, you will learn from your mistakes. Making mistakes comes along with life lessons.

SMART

You can be successful. You are capable of being all that you can be. Set a goal and achieve it. Achieve your short term and long term goals.

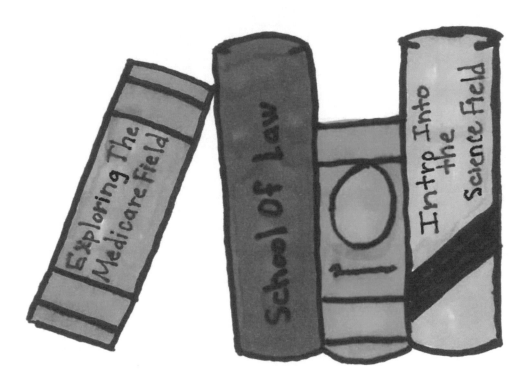

CONFIDENCE

Be confident in everything you do. Stand firm, shoulders
back, and chin up. Confidence is the key to success.

Confidence

DREAM

Follow your dreams. Let nothing stop you. The journey through life has only begun.

STRONG

You are as strong as a mighty giant. Tough, courageous, and brave. You will conquer it all. Maintain your mental health and balance out your life.

SMILE

You have a smile as big as the universe. Smiling is good for the soul. Smile through the good and bad situations you face in life.

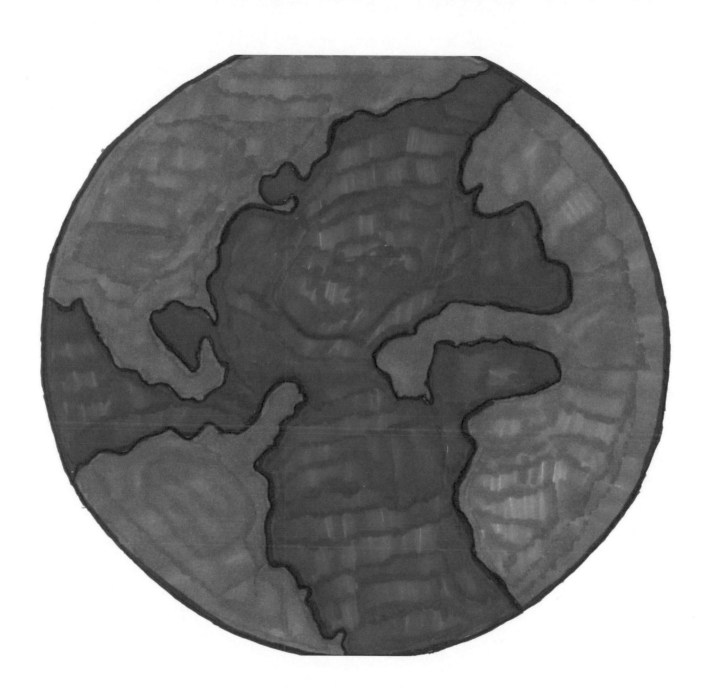

HEART

You have a heart of gold. Be humble, loving, and bold.

EMBRACE

Embrace us with your grace. Create a path that no one will ever forget. Be a leader, hero, and a inspiration to your peers. Touch the hearts of those you inspire.

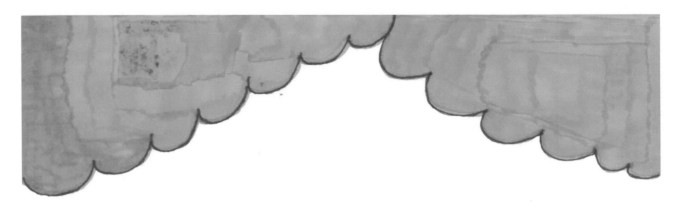

LOVE

Love yourself. You are the best thing that can happen to you. Have self-love, self-control, and self-care. Remember you come first in any decision regarding your happiness or goals. Overcome obstacles and never give up.

SKIN

Your skin is soft. Your glow is outstanding.
Like a diamond, you are shining.

"Glow Girl Magic"

COMPLEXION

Your black is beautiful. You light up like rays in the sky.

SELF ESTEEM

You are special. You are talented. You are important. You can do it.

BELIEVE IN YOU

You are smart. You are confident. You are valuable. You are beautiful. You were created to be different. You are extraordinary. You are one of a kind. You are morale. You are unique. You are the future. You are a high school graduate. You are a leader. You are a doctor. You are a lawyer. You are a nurse. You can save lives. You are a soldier. You are a policeman. You are a firefighter. You are a paramedic. You do matter. You are an educator. You are an engineer. You are a scientist. You are an entrepreneur. You are a hero. You are a President. You are a Senator. You are a State Governor. You are a Judge. You are a public speaker. You are a news reporter. You are an inventor. You are a designer. You are a college graduate. You are a famous athlete. You are a famous musician. You are a trendsetter. You can someday change the world. You are important.

Always love and respect yourself.

DEDICATED TO

My son, Jayden

&

The African American Youth Community

RIP *to the Inspirational Legends*

*RIP to my African American KINGZ & QUEENZ who
lost their lives at the hands of tragic times*

*Remember "**WE DO MATTER** "*

Printed in the United States
By Bookmasters